MY
LIFE
Story

MY LIFE Story

MY MEMORIES OF THE

PAST, PRESENT, AND THOUGHTS

FOR THE FUTURE

GUIDED PROMPTS TO HELP TELL YOUR STORY

chartwell
books

What is your life's story? Would you be able to tell it to your family or friends? Could you even tell it to yourself?

In this journal you'll find *hundreds* of prompts designed to inspire you to sit down and discover the story of your life, especially the chapters and scenes that may have been forgotten over time. Is your favorite color the same now as it was when you were a child? Is your favorite food the same now as when you were a child? What is still on your bucket list that you want to do first? Questions like these and more help untangle the mystery that is you, to reconnect with the parts of yourself that you may have shuttered away for one reason or another, and, hopefully, to fall in love with yourself again.

The prompts inside ask questions ranging from lighthearted to deeply profound to help you recreate the narrative of your life. These questions, no matter how difficult, are best answered with full breadth rather than simple, to-the-point responses. This is how you will be most fulfilled by this journal and leave behind a fully realized record of your adventures.

To know yourself is to know others; to create empathy, compassion, and care for yourself is to do the same for others. Use this journal as an excellent companion to your gratitude, empathy, or self-care practices.

Every life story has highs and lows, ebbs and flows. We hope this journal reveals more peaks than valleys and helps you draft future pages of your story to feature more brightness than darkness.

CHAPTER ONE

The First Years

Welcome to a world
filled with wonder!
It's ready and waiting
for you to explore.

"A NEW BABY IS LIKE THE
BEGINNING OF ALL THINGS—
WONDER, HOPE, A DREAM OF
POSSIBILITIES."

—EDA J. LESHAN

ARE THERE DETAILS ABOUT YOUR BIRTH YOU WISH YOU KNEW BUT CURRENTLY DON'T?

HOW DID YOUR PARENTS REMEMBER YOUR BIRTH AND WITH WHAT TONE DO THEY RETELL THE STORY?

WERE ANY OF THE BABY ITEMS YOU USED FAMILY HEIRLOOMS, OR SOMETHING PASSED DOWN
THROUGH GENERATIONS?

WHAT HAVE YOUR PARENTS OR FAMILY SAID WAS YOUR LEAST FAVORITE BABY ITEM?

WERE YOU A BABY WHO WAS PRONE TO TEARS OR PRONE TO SMILING AND LAUGHING AND WHY?

WHO DOES YOUR FAMILY SAY WAS YOUR FAVORITE PERSON AND WHY DO YOU THINK THAT WAS?

WHAT IS THE EARLIEST DREAM YOU CAN REMEMBER HAVING?

WHAT WAS THE FIRST FOOD YOU ATE THAT YOU REMEMBER ENJOYING AND CAN YOU RECALL WHY?

HOW OLD YOU WERE WHEN YOU FIRST SLEPT THROUGH THE NIGHT?

_____

_____

_____

_____

_____

_____

_____

_____

_____

_____

_____

_____

WHAT DID YOU NEED IN YOUR BED TO HELP YOU SLEEP?

_____

_____

_____

_____

_____

_____

_____

_____

_____

_____

_____

_____

_____

_____

_____

WHAT WAS YOUR FAVORITE TOY AS A CHILD AND WHY DO YOU THINK IT RESONATED WITH YOU?

WHO WAS THE FIRST PERSON TO MEET YOU OUTSIDE OF YOUR IMMEDIATE FAMILY? HOW DID YOU RESPOND?

WHAT WAS THE FIRST SONG EVER SUNG TO YOU OR YOUR FAVORITE SONG AS A BABY?

WHAT DID YOUR PARENTS DRESS YOU UP AS FOR YOUR FIRST HALLOWEEN?

WHAT WAS YOUR FIRST WORD AND WHO WAS THERE TO HEAR IT? HOW DID THEY RESPOND?

WHAT DID YOUR PARENTS SAY WAS YOUR LEAST FAVORITE FOOD AS A BABY?

DID YOUR PARENTS EXPERIENCE ANY MAJOR SCARES WHEN YOU WERE A BABY?

HOW DO YOU THINK YOUR BIRTH ORDER AFFECTED THE WAY YOU WERE PARENTED IN YOUR EARLY YEARS?

WHICH OF YOUR BABY ITEM DO YOU WISH YOU COULD GIVE TO A CHILD IN YOUR LIFE?

WERE YOU CARED FOR BY A COMMUNITY OF FAMILY AND FRIENDS OR JUST YOUR IMMEDIATE FAMILY?

WHAT WAS YOUR PARENTS' GREATEST HOPE FOR YOU WHEN YOU WERE BORN?

CHAPTER TWO

Childhood

The years of the "whys," or when our curiosity sparks and hopefully thrives, not dies.

"JUST LIKE A PLANT NEEDS LIGHT AND SPACE TO GROW, A CHILD NEEDS LOVE AND FREEDOM TO UNFOLD."
—*SIGRID LEO*

DESCRIBE YOUR MOST FAVORITE DAY YOU REMEMBER EXPERIENCING AS A CHILD.

WHAT PLACE OR ITEM PIQUED YOUR INTEREST THE MOST AND WERE YOU ABLE TO EXPLORE IT?

WHERE WAS THE FARTHEST PLACE FROM HOME YOU TRAVELED TO AND DID YOU ENJOY IT THERE?

WHAT WAS YOUR FAVORITE BOOK TO READ OR TO BE READ TO YOU AND WHY?

WHAT WAS THE FIRST SUBJECT YOU LEARNED THAT REALLY CAUGHT YOUR INTEREST AND WHY?

WHAT QUESTION DID YOU ASK AS A CHILD WHOSE ANSWER LEFT YOU THE MOST UNSATISFIED?

WERE YOU THE TYPE OF CHILD WHO WOULD RESEARCH ANSWERS YOURSELF OR ACCEPT WHAT SOMEONE ELSE SAID?

WAS THERE A TIME OF DAY YOUR FAMILY WOULD BE MOST WILLING TO ANSWER YOUR QUESTIONS?

WHAT WAS THE COLOR SCHEME OF YOUR CHILDHOOD BEDROOM AND DID YOU LIKE IT?

DID YOU LIKE THE FIRST TEACHER YOU REMEMBER? WHY OR WHY NOT?

WHERE DID YOU WANT TO VISIT MOST AS A KID AND WHY?

DID THE SUN OR THE MOON HOLD THE MOST FASCINATION FOR YOU AS A CHILD AND WHY?

WHAT IS YOUR MOST FAVORITE EXPERIMENT YOU CONDUCTED AS A CHILD AND WHY?

DESCRIBE HOW YOU WOULD'VE DECORATED YOUR CHILDHOOD ROOM IF YOUR PARENTS
WOULD'VE LET YOU.

_____

_____

_____

_____

_____

_____

_____

_____

_____

_____

_____

_____

_____

_____

_____

_____

_____

_____

_____

_____

_____

_____

_____

_____

_____

_____

_____

_____

_____

_____

LIST YOUR TOP-FIVE FAVORITE SMELLS THAT YOU REMEMBER FROM YOUR CHILDHOOD.

DESCRIBE WHAT YOUR FAVORITE OUTFIT WAS TO WEAR WHEN YOU WERE A KID.

DESCRIBE WHAT YOU REMEMBER AS THE LEAST FAVORITE FOOD YOU EVER ATE AS A CHILD.

WHAT WAS THE FIRST RECORDED SONG YOU EVER REMEMBER HEARING AND HOW DID IT MAKE YOU FEEL?

WHAT WAS YOUR FAVORITE GAME THAT YOU PLAYED AS A CHILD AND WHAT WERE THE RULES?

WHO WAS YOUR VERY FIRST BEST FRIEND AND WHY DO YOU THINK YOU CLICKED WITH THEM?

WHO WAS YOUR VERY FIRST NEMESIS AND WHY DO YOU THINK YOU COULDN'T GET ALONG?

WHAT'S THE PET YOU DIDN'T HAVE AS A CHILD THAT YOU WISH YOU COULD'VE HAD AND WHY?

RANK YOUR CHILDHOOD CLASSES FROM LEAST BORING TO MOST EXCITING AND EXPLAIN THE RANKING.

WHAT WAS YOUR MOST CHERISHED MEMORABILIA YOU HAVE OR WISHED YOU STILL HAD
FROM CHILDHOOD?

WHAT WAS THE GREATEST DISCOVERY OR REALIZATION OF YOUR CHILDHOOD THAT STILL RESONATES
FOR YOU?

CHAPTER THREE

Early Adolescence

It is the best of times, it is the worst of times, it is the most confusing of times.

"WHY FIT IN WHEN YOU WERE BORN TO STAND OUT?"
—*DR. SEUSS*

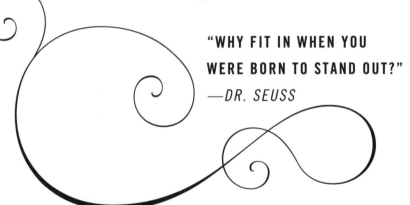

LIST FIVE OBJECTS YOU REMEMBER FROM ONE OF YOUR MIDDLE SCHOOL/JUNIOR HIGH SCHOOL CLASSES AND DESCRIBE THEM.

WHAT WAS A NEW SUBJECT YOU LEARNED THAT MADE YOU EXCITED ABOUT THE TOPIC?

WHAT WOULD BE A TYPICAL BREAKFAST YOU ATE BEFORE YOU STARTED YOUR SCHOOL DAY?

WHAT WAS A CHORE YOU ENJOYED DOING AND A CHORE YOU DETESTED DOING?

LIST THREE THINGS YOU CONTINUED USING AFTER LEAVING PRIMARY SCHOOL AND WHY.

WHO WAS YOUR FAVORITE MUSICAL ARTIST AT THIS TIME AND WHY?

DID YOU REMAIN CLOSE WITH YOUR BEST FRIEND FROM PRIMARY SCHOOL OR DID YOU CHANGE SOCIAL CIRCLES?

WHAT WERE THE TOP HOUSE RULES DURING THE EARLY ADOLESCENT YEARS AND DID THEY CHANGE FROM CHILDHOOD?

HOW OLD WERE YOU WHEN YOU REALIZED YOU WERE GOING THROUGH PUBERTY AND HOW DID YOU FEEL?

WHAT WAS YOUR FAVORITE SCHOOL FIELD TRIP AND WHAT MADE IT SO SPECIAL?

WHAT WAS THE FIRST BOOK WITHOUT PICTURES DID YOU READ THAT YOU TRULY ENJOYED?

WHAT TASK DID YOUR PARENTS GAVE YOU THAT SIGNALED THEY RECOGNIZED YOU WEREN'T A YOUNG KID ANYMORE?

_____
_____
_____
_____
_____
_____
_____
_____
_____
_____
_____
_____
_____
_____
_____
_____
_____
_____
_____
_____
_____
_____
_____
_____
_____
_____
_____
_____

WHAT IS A MEMORY THAT MAKES YOU LAUGH NOW BUT AT THE TIME WAS DEEPLY EMBARRASSING?

WHAT WERE THE EXTRACURRICULAR ACTIVITIES YOU PARTICIPATED IN AND WHICH WAS YOUR FAVORITE?

IF YOU WENT TO A SCHOOL DANCE, DESCRIBE THE DECORATIONS FOR THE MOST MEMORABLE ONE YOU ATTENDED.

WHAT WAS YOUR FAVORITE EXPERIENCE IN YOUR LEAST FAVORITE MIDDLE/JUNIOR HIGH SCHOOL CLASS?

HOW DID YOU TRAVEL TO AND FROM SCHOOL? DESCRIBE A MEMORABLE EXPERIENCE DURING ONE YOUR TRAVELS.

WHAT WERE YOUR TOP-FIVE FAVORITE SONGS TO LISTEN TO DURING YOUR EARLY ADOLESCENCE?

DESCRIBE WHAT YOUR IDEAL BOOK BAG WOULD'VE BEEN IF YOU COULD'VE HAD IT.

HOW LONG WERE YOUR CLASSES AND DID YOU THINK THEM TOO LONG OR NOT LONG ENOUGH?

WHAT WAS YOUR MOST ELABORATE EXCUSE FOR WHY YOU COULDN'T COMPLETE AN ASSIGNMENT?

FOR YOU, WHAT WAS THE BIGGEST DIFFERENCE BETWEEN PRIMARY SCHOOL AND
MIDDLE/JUNIOR HIGH SCHOOL?

WHAT IS SOMETHING YOU WERE PEER PRESSURED INTO DOING THAT YOU ENDED UP
BEING HAPPY YOU DID?

WHAT IS A TALENT, SKILL, OR INTEREST YOU STARTED TO CULTIVATE DURING THIS TIME?

IF YOU HAD YOUR FIRST CRUSH DURING THIS TIME, WHY DID THIS PERSON APPEAL TO YOU?

DESCRIBE A MOMENT WHEN YOU FELT THE MOST CONFIDENT DURING YOUR EARLY ADOLESCENCE.

RECALL SOMETHING YOU STARTED THAT YOU WERE SURE WOULDN'T WORK OUT BUT THE RESULT WAS FANTASTIC.

DESCRIBE A FAVORITE GROUP PROJECT YOU COMPLETED AND WHO PARTICIPATED WITH YOU.

RECALL THE FIVE MOST POPULAR KIDS IN YOUR SCHOOL AND DESCRIBE WHY YOU THINK THEY WERE.

DID YOU WISH YOU HAD A DIFFERENT FRIEND GROUP IN MIDDLE/JUNIOR HIGH SCHOOL?
WHY OR WHY NOT?

WHO IS SOMEONE YOU WISH YOU WOULD'VE GOTTEN TO KNOW BETTER BUT HADN'T
BECAUSE OF PEER PRESSURE?

HOW SUPPORTIVE WAS YOUR FAMILY IN LETTING YOU PURSUE NEW INTEREST DURING THIS TIME?

WHAT WERE SOME SELF-INFLICTED BARRIERS THAT KEPT YOU FROM HAVING THE IDEAL MIDDLE/HIGH SCHOOL EXPERIENCE?

DESCRIBE THE FIRST TIME A BELIEF YOU HELD WAS CHALLENGED. HOW DID IT MAKE YOU FEEL?

WHEN WAS THE FIRST TIME YOU REALIZED YOUR PARENTS DIDN'T ACTUALLY KNOW EVERYTHING?

DO YOU THINK YOU WERE CLOSER TO OR FURTHER AWAY FROM YOUR INTERNAL
TRUTH DURING THIS TIME?

WHAT WAS THE VERY FIRST PURCHASE YOU REMEMBER MAKING WITH YOUR OWN MONEY?

WHAT WAS THE NUMBER-ONE FILM/TELEVISION SHOW/SONG WHEN YOU TURNED THIRTEEN
AND DID YOU LIKE IT?

WHO WAS THE MOST SUPPORTIVE PERSON FOR YOU DURING THIS TIME AND WHY DO YOU THINK SO?

RECALL AN EXPERIENCE THAT EXEMPLIFIES YOUR MIDDLE/JUNIOR HIGH SCHOOL YEARS AND
DESCRIBE HOW YOU FEEL ABOUT IT.

CHAPTER FOUR

The Teenage Years

Say goodbye to the child you were and lay the foundation for the adult you'll become.

"BEFORE YOU ACT, LISTEN. BEFORE YOU REACT, THINK. BEFORE YOU SPEND, EARN. BEFORE YOU CRITICIZE, WAIT. BEFORE YOU PRAY, FORGIVE. BEFORE YOU QUIT, TRY."

—*ERNEST HEMINGWAY*

WHAT WAS THE HEAVIEST TEXTBOOK YOU HAD DURING HIGH SCHOOL AND DID YOU ENJOY THE SUBJECT?

DESCRIBE THE OUTFIT YOU WORE FOR YOUR FIRST DAY OF HIGH SCHOOL.

DID YOU HAVE A JOB AS A TEEN? IF SO, DID YOU ENJOY IT?

WHAT BODY PART OR FUNCTION CONSISTENTLY BETRAYED YOU THE MOST DURING PUBERTY?

WHAT IS A CLASS YOU DREADED THAT YOU ENDED UP LOVING?

WHAT WAS THE FIRST ARGUMENT YOU REMEMBER WINNING AGAINST YOUR PARENTS?

WHAT WAS A FAD OF YOUR TEENAGE YEARS AND HOW ENTHUSIASTICALLY DID YOU PARTICPATE IN **IT?**

GIVE A HEAD-TO-TOE DESCRIPTION OF YOUR FAVORITE TEENAGE OUTFIT AND HOW
DID IT MAKE YOU FEEL?

IF YOU WERE ABLE TO DATE, DESCRIBE YOUR PARTNER AND WHAT MOST ATTRACTED YOU TO THEM.

WHAT IS SOMETHING YOU TRIED AS A TEENAGER THAT YOU'RE GLAD YOU DID?

RANK YOUR HIGH SCHOOL SCHEDULE FROM LEAST TO MOST EXCITING CLASS AND DESCRIBE WHY.

DO YOU THINK YOUR PERSONALITY REMAINED CONSISTENT WHEN YOU TRANSITIONED FROM PREADOLESCENCE TO ADOLESCENCE?

IN WHAT WAYS DID YOUR SOCIAL CLIQUE CHANGE ONCE YOU ENTERED HIGH SCHOOL?

DID YOU START SOMETHING NEW ONCE YOU ENTERED HIGH SCHOOL THAT YOU HAD ALWAYS WANTED TO TRY?

HOW DID THE PERCEPTION OF ROMANCE SHIFT FOR YOU ONCE YOU BECAME A TEENAGER?

DESCRIBE AN EMOTION YOU REMEMBER EXPERIENCING FOR THE FIRST TIME AS A TEENAGER.

DID YOUR SOCIAL CAPITAL RISE OR FALL ONCE YOU ENTERED HIGH SCHOOL?

DID YOUR MODE OF TRANSPORTATION CHANGE ONCE YOU BECAME A TEENAGER?

AS A TEENAGER, WHAT CAREER DID YOU WANT TO HAVE AND WHY?

WHAT WAS YOUR FIRST EXPERIENCE OF BEING SOMEWHERE WITHOUT ADULT SUPERVISION AND HOW DID YOU FEEL?

DID EXPERIENCES IN HIGH SCHOOL LAY THE FOUNDATION FOR HOW YOU INTERACTED WITH PEOPLE GOING FORWARD?

WHAT SOMETHING YOU DID THAT BY ALL REASON SHOULDN'T HAVE WORKED OUT BUT DID?

WHAT WAS YOUR MOST SIGNIFICANT RELATIONSHIP DURING THIS TIME, WHETHER ROMANTIC, PLATONIC, OR FAMILIAL?

WHAT WAS SOMETHING YOU LOVED AS A CHILD THAT YOU COULD NO LONGER STAND AS A TEENAGER?

WAS THERE SOMETHING YOU HAD TO LET GO OF AS A TEENAGER THAT YOU REGRETTED?

WHAT WAS SOMETHING YOU COULD DO AS A KID THAT YOU WISHED TEENAGERS COULD DO WITHOUT CRITIQUE?

DESCRIBE THE PLACE WHERE YOU FELT YOU COULD MOST BE YOURSELF.

WHAT WAS YOUR DREAM CAR AS A TEENAGER AND WERE YOU ABLE TO GET IT IN REAL LIFE?

WHAT WAS SOMETHING YOU WERE FORBIDDEN TO DO AS A TEENAGER THAT YOU DID ANYWAY AND WHY?

WHAT ROLE DID YOU PLAY IN YOUR FRIEND GROUP AND DO YOU THINK IT FIT YOUR PERSONALITY?

DID YOUR FRIENDS' PARENTS THINK YOU WERE A GOOD OR A BAD INFLUENCE? WERE THEY RIGHT?

WHICH ONE OF YOUR FRIENDS DID YOUR PARENTS LIKE THE MOST AND LEAST. WAS THAT OPINION FAIR?

WHAT DID YOU DO AS A TEEN THAT MADE YOU THE MOST DISAPPOINTED IN YOURSELF?

DESCRIBE A TIME WHERE YOU CONVINCED A FRIEND NOT TO MAKE A POOR DECISION.

DESCRIBE SOMETHING THAT WAS SO COOL WHEN YOU WERE A TEENAGER THAT TEENAGERS TODAY WOULDN'T CONSIDER COOL.

LIST FIVE PLACES WHERE YOU WANTED TO LIVE AFTER HIGH SCHOOL AND WHY THEY APPEALED TO YOU.

IDENTIFY THREE GOALS YOU HAD AS A TEENAGER THAT YOU HAVE ACCOMPLISHED.

WHAT IS SOMETHING YOU WISH YOU HAD DONE AS A TEENAGER THAT YOU COULDN'T DO?

WAS THE PERCEPTION PEOPLE HAD OF YOU AS A TEENAGER FAIR OR UNFAIR?

WAS YOUR TEENAGE EXPERIENCE WHAT YOU ENVISIONED IT WOULD BE FROM
WHEN YOU WERE YOUNGER?

CHAPTER FIVE

Early Adulthood

When we realize there is no manual for living, everyone makes it up as they go along.

"I REALIZED THAT I DON'T HAVE TO BE PERFECT. ALL I HAVE TO DO IS SHOW UP AND ENJOY THE MESSY, IMPERFECT, AND BEAUTIFUL JOURNEY OF MY LIFE."

—*KERRY WASHINGTON*

DESCRIBE THE VERY FIRST BEDROOM YOU HAD ONCE YOU MOVED OUT OF YOUR CHILDHOOD HOME.

WHAT WAS THE FIRST ITEM YOU BOUGHT THAT YOU COULDN'T PURCHASE WHEN YOU WERE A CHILD?

WHAT WAS THE GREATEST NUMBER OF ROOMMATES YOU'VE EVER HAD, AND DID YOU
GET ALONG WITH THEM?

WAS YOUR FIRST JOB INTERVIEW AS AN ADULT FOR A DREAM POSITION YOU'VE ALWAYS WANTED?

IDENTIFY THE FIVE BIGGEST DIFFERENCE BETWEEN WHAT YOU THOUGHT ADULTHOOD WAS DURING CHILDHOOD AND WHAT IT IS.

WHAT ARE THREE HABITS YOU HATED IN YOUR PARENTS THAT YOU'VE FOUND YOURSELF ADOPTING?

LIST TEN REASONS WHY YOU WOULD MAKE THE BEST ROMANTIC PARTNER FOR SOMEONE.

DO YOU THINK YOUR MUSICAL TASTES HAVE CHANGED FROM WHEN YOU WERE A TEENAGER TO THIS TIME?

WHAT FILM, THEATER PRODUCTION, BOOK, OR SONG BEST DESCRIBES THIS ERA OF YOUR LIFE AND WHY?

WHAT ARE SOME SIMILARITIES BETWEEN YOUR EARLY ADULTHOOD AND THAT OF YOUR PARENTS?

ARE YOU STILL FRIENDS WITH PEOPLE FROM YOUR CHILDHOOD OR TEENAGE YEARS?

WHAT ARE THREE THINGS THAT HAVE REMAINED CONSISTENT ABOUT YOU FROM
CHILDHOOD TO THIS POINT?

HOW PREPARED DID YOU FEEL WHEN YOU FIRST STARTED LIVING OUTSIDE OF YOUR CHILDHOOD HOME?

WHAT ARE TEN TRAITS POTENTIAL ROMANTIC PARTNERS MUST HAVE FOR YOU TO PURSUE A RELATIONSHIP WITH THEM?

HOW DID YOU FEEL WHEN YOU RECEIVED YOUR FIRST PAYCHECK AS AN ADULT?

HAVE THE QUALITIES YOU FOUND ATTRACTIVE IN SOMEONE CHANGED OR REMAINED THE SAME FROM WHEN YOU WERE YOUNGER?

WHAT IS A FOOD YOU USED TO HATE AS A CHILD THAT YOU LOVE AS AN ADULT?

ARE YOU CLOSER TO YOUR BIOLOGICAL FAMILY OR YOUR FRIENDS AND HOW DO YOU FEEL ABOUT THAT?

WHAT DOES YOUR IDEAL HOME FEEL LIKE AND HOW CLOSE ARE YOU TO CREATING THAT ATMOSPHERE?

WHAT IS THE MOST DOMINANT COLOR IN YOUR WARDROBE, AND DOES IT MATCH YOUR PERSONALITY?

WHAT IS SOMETHING YOU VOWED YOU'D NEVER DO AS A CHILD THAT YOU ACTUALLY LOVE DOING NOW?

HOW LONG DOES IT TAKE FOR SOMEONE TO GET TO KNOW THE REAL YOU AFTER MEETING?

WHAT ARE THE TOP THREE THINGS YOU'D LIKE TO IMPROVE ABOUT YOURSELF DURING THIS TIME?

WHEN WAS THE LAST TIME YOU LOOKED AT THE STARS IN THE SKY?

DESCRIBE FIVE SOUNDS THAT PUT YOU IN A CALM AND PLEASANT HEADSPACE.

CHAPTER SIX

Adulthood

Here's to implementing what we've learned and paying the knowledge forward so the next generation can step into a brighter future.

"MY MISSION IN LIFE IS NOT MERELY TO SURVIVE, BUT TO THRIVE; AND TO DO SO WITH SOME PASSION, SOME COMPASSION, SOME HUMOR, AND SOME STYLE." —*MAYA ANGELOU*

WHAT IS SOMETHING NEW THAT YOU WANT TO TRY BUT YOU STILL HAVEN'T YET?

WHAT HAS BEEN A PROFOUND LESSON YOU'VE LEARNED DURING THIS TIME THAT COULDN'T REGISTER WHEN YOU WERE YOUNGER?

WHAT IS A LINGERING QUESTION FROM YOUR CHILDHOOD THAT YOU'RE STILL TRYING TO ANSWER?

HAVE YOU CREATED A BUCKET LIST? IF SO, HOW MANY ITEMS HAVE YOU CROSSED OFF SO FAR?

WHAT WERE THE THREE MILESTONES THAT SIGNIFIED "MADE IT" FOR YOU AS AN ADULT WHEN
YOU WERE YOUNGER?

HOW DO YOU ENSURE THE PERSON YOU CURRENTLY ARE ALIGNS WITH THE PERSON YOU WANT TO BE?

WHAT'S THE UNIVERSAL ENERGY YOU CURRENTLY ATTRACT AND HOW DOES IT MATCH THE ENERGY YOU'D LIKE TO RECEIVE?

LIST FIVE HABITS YOU ARE PROUD OF YOURSELF FOR ADOPTING THAT YOU DIDN'T
THINK YOU COULD.

LIST SEVEN WORDS YOU ASSOCIATE WITH YOURSELF AND DESCRIBE HOW YOU FEEL ABOUT THEM.

WHAT IS A LESSON YOU LEARNED AS A CHILD THAT YOU REALIZE YOU MUST UNLEARN AS AN ADULT?

WHAT IS A CURRENT PIECE OF TECHNOLOGY YOU WISH HAD BEEN AROUND WHEN YOU WERE A CHILD?

ARE YOU MORE OR LESS NOSTALGIC FOR YOUR CHILDHOOD THAN YOU THOUGHT YOU WOULD BE?

WHAT IS A HOME IMPROVEMENT PROJECT YOU COMPLETED THAT MADE YOU FEEL LIKE THE NEXT BOB VILA?

WHAT IS A LESSON YOU WISH YOUR PARENTS HAD TAUGHT THAT YOU HAD TO DISCOVER
ON YOUR OWN?

WHAT IS YOUR DREAM VACATION AND IS IT THE SAME OR DIFFERENT FROM WHEN YOU WERE YOUNGER?

WHAT IS A CHERISHED RELATIONSHIP YOU HAVE WITH A YOUNGER PERSON IN YOUR LIFE?

HOW DO YOU THINK YOUR GENERATION HAS HELPED GENERATIONS AFTER YOU BE ABLE TO
SUCCEED IN LIFE?

WHO IS A CHERISHED OLDER PERSON IN YOUR LIFE AND HOW DO YOU CONTINUE LEARNING FROM THEM?

WHAT IS SOMETHING YOU NEVER THOUGHT WOULD HAPPEN IN YOUR LIFE THAT YOU'RE GLAD IT DID?

WHAT IS SOMETHING YOU'D WISH WOULD HAPPEN IN YOUR LIFE AND YOU'RE RELIEVED IT DIDN'T?

IF THERE WAS A CONCERT YOU COULD ATTEND, WHAT WOULD IT BE AND WHY?

DESCRIBE YOUR TOP FIVE FAVORITE SMELLS AND WHY THEY MADE THE LIST.

WHO IS THE GREATEST LOVE OF YOUR LIFE AND DID THAT PERSON KNOW IT?

WHAT ARE THREE ASPECTS OF YOUR LIFE THAT MAKE YOU FEEL THE MOST VULNERABLE?

HOW COMFORTABLE ARE YOU WITH BEING EMOTIONALLY UNCOMFORTABLE AND DO YOU TRY TO AVOID BEING SO?

WHAT IS SOMETHING THAT USED TO CAUSE YOU GREAT ANXIETY BUT NOW YOU
FEEL GREAT CONFIDENCE?

WHAT IS THE HEAVIEST EMOTIONAL BAGGAGE YOU HAVE LET GO SO FAR?

WHAT IS A HURT YOU HAVE UNINTENTIONALLY PASSED DOWN FROM YOU TO YOUNGER PEOPLE
IN YOUR LIFE?

WHAT IS SOMETHING A YOUNGER PERSON INTRODUCED YOU TO THAT YOU ENJOY?

NAME YOUR FIVE FAVORITE FILMS, BOOKS, OR SONGS THAT HAVE COME OUT IN THE LAST TEN YEARS.

WHAT IS A SCIENTIFIC DISCOVERY THAT HAS IMPRESSED YOU THE MOST?

WHAT IS SOMETHING FROM YOUR CHILDHOOD THAT YOU WISH WOULD COME BACK NOW?

WHAT DOES A PEACEFUL DAY LOOK LIKE TO YOU KNOW COMPARED TO TWENTY YEARS AGO?

NAME A NEW ARTIST THAT YOU THINK COULD'VE BEEN SUCCESSFUL WHEN YOU WERE A TEEN.

WHO IS SOMEONE YOU'VE NEVER MET BUT WOULD REALLY LIKE TO SOMEDAY?

WHAT HAS BEEN YOUR CLOSEST BRUSH WITH FAME AND HOW DID IT MAKE YOU FEEL?

WHAT HAS BEEN YOUR GREATEST ACHIEVEMENT AND HOW IS IT DIFFERENT FROM WHAT YOU'D INITIALLY ENVISIONED?

WHO DO YOU CONSIDER HAS BEEN THE MOST SUPPORTIVE PERSON IN YOUR PROFESSIONAL CAREER AND WHY?

WHAT ARE THREE DISCOVERIES YOU HOPE SCIENTISTS WILL MAKE IN YOUR LIFETIME?

Brimming with creative inspiration, how-to projects, and useful information to enrich your everyday life, Quarto Knows is a favorite destination for those pursuing their interests and passions. Visit our site and dig deeper with our books into your area of interest: Quarto Creates, Quarto Cooks, Quarto Homes, Quarto Lives, Quarto Drives, Quarto Explores, Quarto Gifts, or Quarto Kids.

This edition published in 2021 by Chartwell Books,
an imprint of The Quarto Group,
142 West 36th Street, 4th Floor,
New York, NY 10018, USA
T (212) 779-4972 f (212) 779-6058
www.QuartoKnows.com

Previously published in 2020 by Chartwell Books, an imprint of The Quarto Group,
142 West 36th Street, 4th Floor, New York, NY 10018, USA

Chartwell titles are also available at discount for retail, wholesale, promotional, and bulk purchase. For details, contact the special sales manager by email at specialsales@quarto.com or by mail at The Quarto Group, ATTN: Special Sales Manager, 100 Cummings Center, Suite 265D, Beverly, MA 01915, USA.

10 9 8 7 6 5 4 3 2 1

ISBN: 978-0-7858-4037-4

Publisher: Rage Kindelsperger
Creative Director: Laura Drew
Managing Editor: Cara Donaldson
Text: Savannah J. Frierson
Cover Design: Beth Middleworth
Interior Design: Beth Middleworth

Printed in China